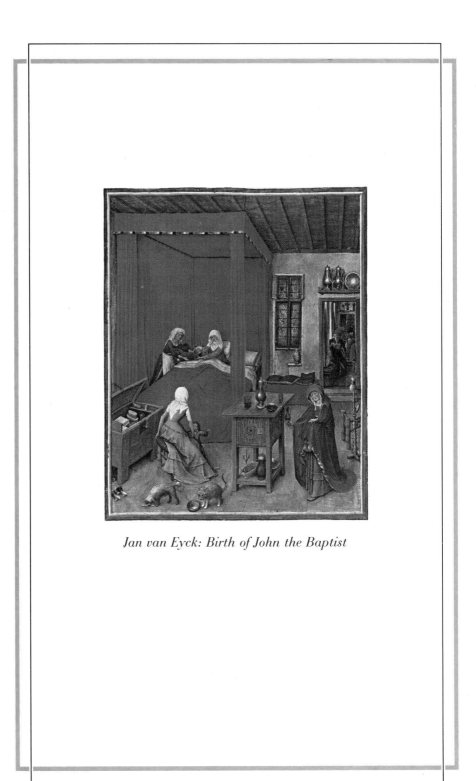

Jan van Eyck: Birth of John the Baptist

On Going To Bed

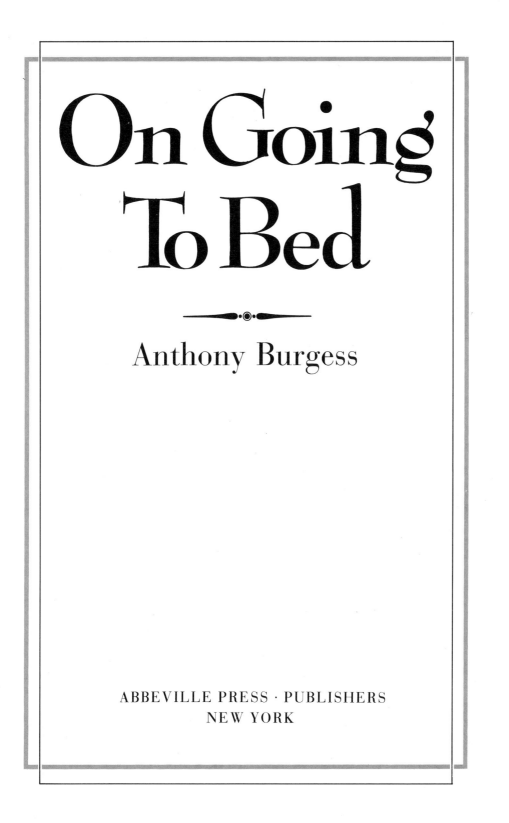

Anthony Burgess

ABBEVILLE PRESS · PUBLISHERS
NEW YORK

THE TEXT OF *ON GOING TO BED*
BY ANTHONY BURGESS WAS DEVELOPED AROUND
AN IDEA BY GABRIELE PANTUCCI

Library of Congress Cataloging in Publication Data
Burgess Anthony
On Going to Bed
1. Beds and bedsteads.   2. Sleeping customs
I. Title
GT450.887   392.36   81-22757
ISBN 0-89659-280-4

First U.S. edition

The text of the illustrated pages
is by the Editors of Rizzoli Editore.

Raphael: Moses Rescued from the Waters

The prophet Moses, who brought us all out of the house of bondage of polytheism and taught us reading, writing and the application of both to contracts and covenants, first presents himself to the public in a basket, or *moïse*, moving towards royal adoption down the river Nile. His sister Miriam wove his boat and, carrying it and its precious burden to the water's edge, probably improvised the first lullaby. It was essential that the potential saviour of his people not cry aloud and thus betray himself to the Egyptian police, who had orders to kill all the Israelite men-children. We cannot doubt that her song had *lulla* or *lolla* or *lalla* in it: the consonant called a liquid, the most soothing sound in the whole inventory, is essential to cradlesongs. Miriam, a virgin destined to be a prophetess, is the first of the great mothers. Eve did nothing for her children except arrange for them to be born in original sin.

The primal bed is a liquid. Moses was launched on the waters for a rebirth, and those waters symbolized the amniotic fluid which, but a short time before, had borne him in the womb. A child's life before birth is one of gentle rocking, and our wise ancestors saw that the rhythm had to be sustained for some time after it. The rocking of the cradle, recalled in the flow of the sea, is one of the basic beats of all music. 'Rocked in the cradle of the deep,' went the old song, and Whitman's *Sea Drift* begins with 'Out of the cradle endlessly rocking.' Sleep is gentle rocking travel along the river of the dark. Not that such rocking could not sometimes partake of wilder and more irregular rhythms, such as those of the wind. A nursery rhyme, probably very old, though our version of it dates back only to the sixteenth century, starts by soothing:

Rockabye baby on the tree-top.
When the wind blows the cradle will rock.

But it ends with a reminder of Eve's gift:

When the bough breaks the cradle will fall –
Down will come cradle and baby and all.

A reminder also to the mother to secure the cradle among boughs not likely to break. Tacitus records that the Germanic tribes of two thousand years back used to put not only babies but old men in cradles among the branches. In our end is our beginning. The very young and very old are equally precious and equally a burden: they cannot dig fields or bear arms. The Egyptian hieroglyphic is the same for infant and ancient. Old men rock in rocking-chairs, sucking their pipes. Babies suck at their bottles. They recognize their kinship, toothless, with slack Churchillian faces.

One of the earliest external, as opposed to maternal, odours known to the primitive child must have been that of wood. The wood chosen for the making of the cradle was traditionally birch, which wards off evil spirits. Elderwood was dangerous since it attracted fairies, who would pinch the baby, sometimes in both senses of the word. The division between lowly and high-born children was marked by the use of wood for the cradles of the first, metal for the latter. A curved shield made an admirable rocker for the son of a military officer: the first

Prince of Wales was presented to his people lying on one. George IV of Great Britain slept in a golden cradle. But none of these noble cradles, whether of gold or silver or steel, were of much use unless they were mounted on rockers. It was the rocking that was important, and rocking seems to have disappeared from the infant regimen. Somebody said that it caused anaemia and damaged the brain. Now children are put in cots, which are miniature prisons complete with bars. There is no movement in their little universe.

And yet even far into adult life we have the best sleep when we are moving: we are back with the infant Moses. When I first voyaged on a troopship I had to learn the skill of putting up a hammock and getting into it; the skills once learned, I never slept better. Now that we no longer travel much by sea, we have to regard the *wagon-lit* as the best way of doing something (viz., moving from A to B, or even to Z) while doing nothing (viz., sleeping). But there is something to be said for sleeping in a near-empty Jumbo jet. A little while ago I flew from Kuala Lumpur to London stretched on a long row of seats with the armrests pulled up, supported by plastic pillows and covered with paper-thin blankets. The sleep was of that intermittent kind which makes almost a conscious pleasure out of it, for the plane dipped and soared in clear air turbulence, and a film was being shown which nobody looked at, except in the metamorphosis of a dream. Its key scene was of an aircraft on fire.

But you cannot beat a *wagon-lit*. There is something in all of us which begrudges sleep – 'Short, oh short then be thy reign and give us to the world again' – and feels cheated to find that we have wakened where we dropped off. Nothing has been achieved except exhaustion, a few silly dreams, the stretching of the bladder and the desiccation of the mouth. On a *wagon-lit* you reach Paris or Barcelona or Rome or Milan. You have been wakened gently at intervals by station lights and guards' whistles, which are as good as having a servant call you to tell you it is not yet time to get up. You have, moreover, been sent to bed like an infant, since you are enclosed in a cell which is set out only for sleep, so sleep you have to. You are in a situation of total irresponsibility: you do not have to drive the train. You are rocked like an infant, but you are performing one of the most adult tasks in the world – getting from one place to another.

But there are occasions when the rhythm of the cradle turns to hurtful music. This is when we go to bed drunk, and the structure seems to move, from top to bottom, not from side to side. The bottom of the bed rises towards us, and we know with queasy intuition that we have to get up for a painful purgation. One of the unkindest sensations that life offers is the waking, totally sober, in a ship's bunk and finding that one seems to have been drinking. It makes one believe in original sin.

Piero della Francesca: An altar polyptych showing a miracle of St Anthony

Cradles

Doctors and psychologists have reached no conclusion as to why rocking quietens a new-born baby; they merely confirm that rocking is effective – to the great relief of all parents and nurses. This explains why the cradle goes back to our earliest history, or rather pre-history.

The shape of cradles has varied greatly, ranging from the primitive hollowed tree-trunk of proto-historic cultures, to such cradles as the very ornate walnut Brustolon cradle (now in the Museo Horne in Florence), the cradle from Valtellina, which combines centuries of popular tradition, and the 16th-century cradle to be found in the Casa Cavassa Museum at Saluzzo. Between simplicity and elaboration come the functional incubator and the cradle created for Napoleon Bonaparte's son who, under the title of Duke of Reichstadt, was brought up at the court in Vienna.

Wood is the material most often used, followed by wicker, which was used in 17th-century Holland (see the painting by Maes), then in various parts of Europe in the 19th century (see the design for a French cradle) and in our own times. Curved rockers usually set a cradle rocking, but there are examples (as in Syrian houses) of swinging cradles, suspended by thongs or cords. Cradles also appear as toys, intended to hold dolls; and so we complete the circle and return to childhood.

A 19th-century cradle from Valtellina, Italy

An early 16th-century Italian cradle

A suspended cradle in a house in Palmyra, Syria

An incubator in use at a maternity hospital in Milan

Nicholas Maes: Young Woman with Child (detail)

A doll in a cradle
once belonging to
Queen Victoria

The cradle
made for the
Duke of Reichstadt

A design for a French 19th-century
wicker cradle

A walnut Brustolon cradle,
probably late 18th century

To be born in bed

Our Lord was content with a little straw and a manger. Some have their first glimpse of the world from inside a taxi, a lift, an airport lounge. But these are the exceptions: most people, now and in the past, have been born in bed. And they will, no doubt, continue to be born in that way — probably in one of those gadget-like instruments of torture which modern hospitals call delivery beds.

Parallel with change in the design of beds goes change in style for the 'scenography' of birth. We have only to look at scenes of birth in Renaissance paintings, where whatever the event depicted, it was customary to give it a contemporary setting, to see how very different things were then. For example, in the picture by the Master of the Life of Mary (today in Munich's Alte Pinakothek), in Birth of the Virgin by the Prato Master and in the painting by Lambert Sustris (now in the Galleria Borghese in Rome), crowds of ladies, servants and even strangers comfort, amuse, compliment and presumably disturb the woman in labour.

The technique of wrapping newborn babies in swaddling bands is clearly shown in the fresco at the Castle of Roccabianca (Parma), dated circa 1480 and inspired by the tenth story on day ten in the Decameron, and also in The Adoration of the Magi, by the Frenchman Georges de La Tour, which now hangs in the Louvre.

Master of the Life of Mary: Birth of the Virgin (detail)

Anonymous: The Life of Griselda

Lambert Sustris: A Birth

Master of Prato:
Birth of the Virgin

Georges de La Tour:
Adoration of the Magi
(detail)

A bed for all occasions

A bed is not a living-room; but it can be something similar, and perhaps something more. It is a piece of furniture with many functions around which all or part of a family's life can revolve. So the bed in everyday life has come to symbolize comfort and relaxation, whether in the form of stretching out to take a little rest, or of reclining in one's bed to receive guests, as ladies did in the 18th century.

This characteristic comfort, extending even to mealtimes, was thoroughly familiar to the ancients, as witness Egyptian paintings on the stele of the Pharaoh Amenemhat (12th dynasty, about 2000 BC) and the painting in the Vatican Museum, inspired by the story of Dido and Aeneas.

For children the bed is a symbol of belonging and love, which is why they try to coax or wangle their way into the bed of their parents. For them, too, the bed is associated with another act of love, the feeding of a child, which inspired the illustration Baby's Breakfast. *And the bed can mean still other things for a child: a little table on which to eat breakfast under the watchful gaze of two playmates, or a quiet corner in which to say one's prayers.*

Finally, what could be better than waking up in a soft bed on the morning after a delightful ball, there to cast an inquisitive eye over the morning's gossip columns?

Anonymous: Banquet of Dido and Aeneas

The stele of Pharaoh Amenemhat: Family Scene

Anonymous: Baby's Breakfast

Anonymous: Morning after the Ball   *Burton Barber: Suspense*

Anon: Children Saying Prayers

The bed of childhood, as opposed to infancy, can be very thorny except when it is time to get up. The worst thing you can threaten a child with is sending him to bed. Yet once he is in bed and asleep the worst cruelty is to drag him out of it. We are sustained by anomalies. Sleep and waking are two opposed kingdoms. We are reluctant to break allegiance to either.

When I was a child I would always cry when I was told it was time for bed. It was not just a matter of having to abandon the lively fireplace and go out into the cold and dark. It was like being sentenced to death and a sure hell after it. In those days bedrooms were never heated, and to take off one's little shirt was like inviting the slash of metal on one's body. The shadows were full of executioners' axes. The quick night prayer, one knew, would yield no comfort. 'If I die before I wake, I pray the Lord my soul to take.' What could this mean except that the causes of premature death lay somehow in sleep itself. If sleep was an imitation of death, the impersonation could all too easily transform itself into an identity. But when I got into the cold lumpy bed I did not die: I was all too horribly alive in a world of monsters.

On the wall, opposite my bed, was a painting of a gipsy woman telling the cards. Attached to the frame was the title *Beware*! This picture was the last thing I saw before putting out the light, but with the putting out of the light and the closing of my eyes it expanded and became a huge door. The door would open to mocking tinny music and disclose a landscape of bones and horse-droppings, brilliantly illuminated by a sort of hellfire. Little men with the faces of dogs would caper and leap and call my name: they wanted me there with them, presumably to kill and bury among the bones and ordure. I would scream and scream and wake to the dark, except for dim lamplight from the street glowing on the gipsy with her cards (had she turned up the nine of spades? I knew nothing then of cartomancy) and the words I had been told spelt out *Beware*!

The habit of nightmares has persisted into adulthood, and the fear of a nightmare still makes me reluctant to go to bed. The nightmares often feature bones and the excrement of animals, and sometimes the excrement becomes animated into a snake. Freud no doubt would explain the persistent symbols, but I have sometimes dreamt of Freud performing such an explication, not very satisfactorily.

Who can talk of the blessing of sleep, especially for lonely and imaginative children, when sleep unlocks so many horrors? Daymares do not exist, and that is why the best sleep is the sleep protected by the light of the morning. It is a terrible crime to drag children from bed in the winter's dawn to send them to school. If a child wishes to stay in bed, even in summer, it is because he has been exhausted by his phantasmal experiences of the night.

The night is a bad time, and that is why black is an evil colour, even among those who call themselves black. No one, however black of skin, thinks of himself as of the colour of the night – the colour of berries or aubergines, perhaps, which are round and living, but never of that abstraction of light which is full of predators and goblins. Apart from the terrible apparitions that lurk in the brain, awaiting the release of sleep, there are the things which happen outside it, even in the most rational household. There are the creaks and stretchings of the furniture, which is wondering whether or not to come alive. There are the other sleeping denizens of the house, who shout strange words out of their dreams or even somnambulate and dare not, for fear of a lethal shock, be wakened from their walking. I remember once staying with a brother and sister who both, about three in the morning, decided to walk at the same time. Miraculously, they did not cross each other's path but independently got on with their business. The boy turned on all the lights he could get at and dealt out four hands for whist on my bed. The girl merely wandered the house laughing and crying out the one word 'Paste!'

There are some bizarre stories about sleepwalking. I think we have all heard of the lady, guest in a great house, who woke in the small hours to hear the breathing and moving of a male presence. On the coverlet she could feel objects being placed in order and with deliberation. She did not dare stir. Wisely she fainted. She came to at dawn to find that the butler had walked in his sleep and laid the table for fourteen on her bed. Lawrence Wright, the bed expert, tells of the baronet in Hampshire who went to bed every night in a shirt and every morning woke stark naked. There was no trace of the garment anywhere. After hundreds of shirts had disappeared in this way, he asked a friend to watch over his sleep. The friend did so and, as the clock struck one, observed the baronet get out of bed, light a candle, and walk out of the room. The friend followed him a fair distance to the stableyard, where the baronet took off his shirt and, using a pitchfork, buried it in a dungheap. He then returned, still fast asleep, to his naked bed.

One morning I got up to find the following verses scrawled in lipstick on my dining-room wall:

> *Let his carbon gnoses be up right*
> *And wak all folowers to his light*

The writing was my own and the lipstick my wife's. Some people talk of the inspiration of sleep and assert that there is great wisdom to be tapped in the unconscious mind. If this couplet is a specimen of this wisdom let me stay conscious. I knew a man who woke up in the night to find he had discovered in sleep the key to the universe. He scrawled on a pad kept on his bedside table the mystical unlocking words. Waking he read them: 'All a matter of demisemiquavers. Make much of this.'

Anecdotes of somnambulism and somniscription are either shameful or amusing, but they should be terrifying. Every child going to his bedroom knows that the laws of the night are on the side of the irrational, and the irrational is usually malignant. What is to stop any one of us from getting up in his sleep, committing murder, and then going back to innocent dreams or irrelevant nightmares? I shall never forget an experience I had in London in 1946. The year is significant, for we were all getting over a world nightmare then and our brains were probably deranged. I went to bed sober in a hotel room and awoke to find myself eating a herring in the apartment of a complete stranger who chatted to me as if I were an old friend. What had I done in the meantime? I did not dare to ask. You can explain this experience in terms of amnesia: I had been behaving normally but now suffered from a gap of memory. But it would not have happened if I had not gone to bed.

Auden wrote: 'Forget the dead, what you've read, all the errors and the terrors of the bed.' A child cannot forget the terrors, which are best dissolved by another human presence, so long as he can be sure that presence is benign. But the terrors come when the child is too old to sleep with his mother and too young to sleep with a lover or mistress. When the lover or spouse arrives the bed will be a place for enacting errors, but, with luck or skill, they can be corrected. There is no cure for nocturnal horrors except not going to bed.

Goya: Saturn

The Etruscan bed

Among the ancient peoples of the Mediterranean basin who used beds not only for sleep but also – and equally – as a primary element of social life, the Etruscans hold a prominent position. In the remains of their civilization, beds appear in frescoes, on vases, on sarcophagi – indeed they appear often enough to support the conjecture that they were objects of religious significance. Comfortable and serene on their couches are the man, the woman, the couple ... Usually they support themselves on their left arm, while the right raises a goblet of wine to accompany the meal, or reaches to caress the companion reclining elegantly close by, as in the famous sarcophagus of the Married Couple, housed in Rome at the Museo di Villa Giulia.

Many kinds of marble are used (for example, the alabaster with a woman's figure in the Museo Etrusco, Volterra), and there are notable differences in the shape of the furniture depicted. This includes the classical couch with wrought legs (found on the polychrome sarcophagus now in the Museo Archeologico, Florence, identified as that of Larthia Seianti and dated 217–147 BC); the 'doric' bed, with decorations which recall a doric metope (see the sarcophagus of the Magistrate in the Museo Archeologico, Tarquinia); and the incredible alcove bed from the Tomb of Reliefs in the necropolis at Cerveteri, so disconcertingly modern in its use of space.

A sarcophagus with female figure

The sarcophagus of the Magistrate 'Laris Pulena'

The polychrome sarcophagus of Larthia Seianti

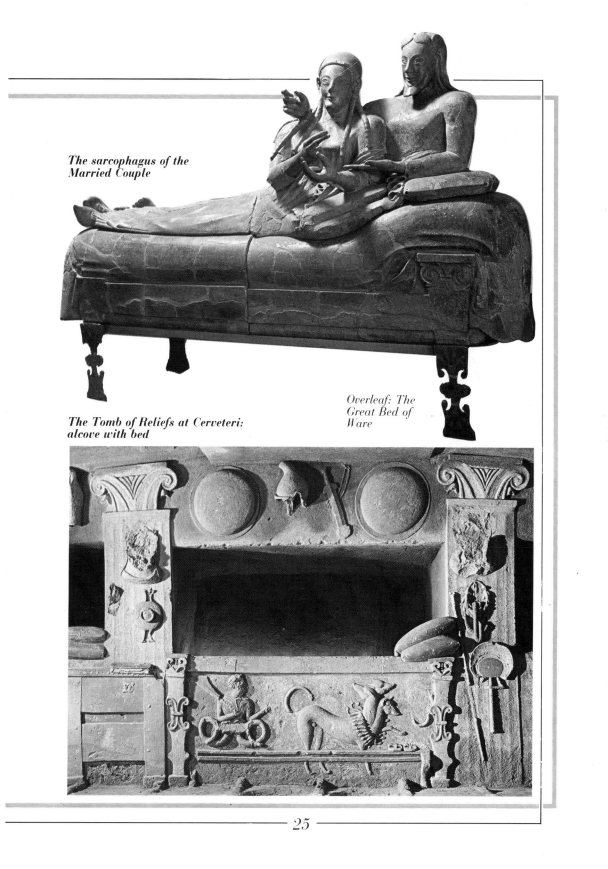

The sarcophagus of the Married Couple

The Tomb of Reliefs at Cerveteri: alcove with bed

Overleaf: The Great Bed of Ware

Style in beds

First a little straw was gathered in a corner, then it was stuffed into a bag to make a mattress. This was the original notion of a bed: something upon which to lie down and rest. Today, respect for ergonomic principles and design puts emphasis again on the bare essentials of a bed; but in the millenia between prehistoric culture and our own, the builders of beds have often taken exactly the opposite view. This was particularly true between the second half of the 17th century and the first half of the 19th. The essential structure became unimportant compared to the individual elements which could enrich a bed: the headboard, the feet, the bedside cupboards, the legs, the canopy. Attention centred on these features, which gave rise to unrestrained use of exotic woods, veneer, brocades and precious velvets, combined in pursuit of luxury and ornament, the aim being to dazzle.

Beds such as these call attention to themselves with a clamorous voice and can be seen as advertising the very rapid changes of taste throughout the reigns of Louis XV and Louis XVI, during the Consulate, and in the First and Second Empire.

Bearing witness to this extravagant flourishing of stylistic invention are the engravings, such as those reproduced here, found in catalogues of designs for furniture and in workmen's inventories.

A military-style day bed

A maple bedstead, amaranthine in colour

A rosewood and thuja bedstead

A French cottage bed

A Louis XV corner bed

Above, below and
bottom left: three
19th-century beds

Below: A style of bed popular
in the reign of Francis I

Eugène Delacroix: Apartment of the Comte de Mornay

Literature tells us little about sleep. The lives of most fictional characters are intermitted at bedtime and resumed with morning tea. Lewis Carroll's two dreambooks are the best-known exception, though Alice's adventures are initiated not in bed but from summer grass and a winter fireside. James Joyce's *Finnegans Wake* is an exception known of but rarely broached by the common reader. All the action takes place in the sleeping mind of the hero, an innkeeper in bed after a busy Saturday night. The materials of his dream, which is a fantastic reshaping of European history, draw on the bed itself, especially the four bedposts traditionally guarded by Matthew, Mark, Luke and John, who are turned into an eight-legged creature called Mamalujo. There are dream episodes dealing with illicit concupiscence, usually incestuous, throughout the tapestry of sleep, but the waking sexual act, between the hero and his wife, is only briefly attempted, and it is a total failure.

But where beds appear in regular literature (*Finnegans Wake* is highly irregular) they are usually the scenes of either sexual triumph or else sexual failure which can be viewed comically. The first famous beds for dalliance occur in Chaucer's *Canterbury Tales*, in the coarse yarns of the Miller and the Carpenter. The tradition of the picaresque novel has much to do with beds in inns and people getting into the wrong bed in the dark. Inn beds were meant for hilarity, not nightmares. The greatest inn bed of all time may still be seen in the Victoria and Albert Museum. It is eleven feet deep and nearly the same wide, and it was installed, in the middle of the sixteenth century, in Ware at the Crown Inn — hence its name, the Great Bed of Ware. Shakespeare mentions it, and so does Ben Jonson. Parties of men and their wives or mistresses would gleefully spend a promiscuous night in it, the thrashing of bare legs making a merry music. The whole world, as a place for surprises and jollity, has been likened to it. We are told that the size of the Great Bed of Ware was not exceptional in Tudor times, that most marital beds were huge and apt for rollicking. The athletics of sex have possibly declined since those days: our marriage beds are small and sometimes chopped into twinhood.

Illicit love may well be conducted in very small beds, and it often is. The marriage bed has a kind of royal status, and its size should be a reflection of this: it is not for casual copulation but for the enactment of the whole drama of marriage, which entails both approximation and withdrawal. It is for quarrels and reconciliations as well as supper and breakfast. It is for curtain lectures of the kind delivered by Mrs Caudle, on which the husband, pretending to be asleep, must turn his back. In Sicily, where the beds are traditionally very big and deep, the conduct of the Mafia may be decreed at length by the don's wife. Destroy the double bed, and you impair government. Kings and prime ministers have been told at length in the dark how to run the state. Without the darkling and confidential wisdom of women in big beds male rulers are nothing.

Twin beds too brashly proclaim the physical functionality of marriage. It is true that the lover's desire to have his mistress sleeping in his arms is best not realized – too much cramp – but it is not up to the makers of twin beds to tell us this so blatantly. To couple and to separate should be tentative, with the implied promise of renewed coupling – a matter of rolling away, not of getting up and going elsewhere, even if the elsewhere be only a few feet distant. If twin beds sound like modern decadence, we have to remember that they go back certainly as far as Charles the Bold of Burgundy and his second wife Isabella in the fifteenth century, and that there has always been a gleam of twin-beddedness in the eyes of the ascetic fathers of the Church. 'Save for the hallowed end of begetting new souls for the kingdom of heaven it is uncleanly for the man and woman to lie together.' Who said that? Origen? Vitellius? Hamlet proclaimed the uncleanliness of the double bed clearly enough: 'Nay, but to live / In the rank sweat of an enseamed bed' (enseamed meant greasy). 'Stewed in corruption, honeying and making love / Over the nasty sty' is meant to be an expression of disgust at the act of incest, but one cannot doubt it goes deeper or less deep. Shakespeare was a queasy-stomached man: one of his reasons for leaving Stratford, so some believe, was to get away from a particular double bed. But see later.

Dr Graham, so Wright tells us in his monumental study of beds, cried out in 1783 on the hurtful custom of 'man and wife continually *pigging* together, in one and the same bed . . . to sleep, to snore, and steam, and do everything else that's indelicate together, three hundred and sixty-five times – every year.' And yet it was Dr Graham who invented the double bed to smother all others, though it was intended only for a dream or prospect of concupiscence rather than the act itself. This was the bed called Celestial, put on exhibition in 1778. It was equipped with 'about 1500 pounds weight of artificial and compound magnets' which revivified slackening sexual vigour and imparted to the bed 'that sweet undulating, tittulating, vibratory, soul-dissolving, marrow-melting motion which on certain critical and important occasions is at once so necessary and so pleasing.' There were also costly Oriental perfumes and 'cherishing vapours'. The structure was not intended for mass-production and domestic use. There was only one Celestial Bed, set up in the Temple of Health in the Adelphi, Strand, and presided over by 'Vestina, the Rosy Goddess of Health,' a blacksmith's daughter named Emma Lyon, eventually to become Lady Hamilton and the mistress of Lord Nelson. It cost fifty pounds a night to sleep in the bed, alone of course: recovering potency was a solitary experience. One can now, by inserting quarters in a slot, have an enlivening refocillation of vigour in American motels: the principle of the magnetic effluvium remains Dr Graham's. Like most great inventors he died poor.

M. di Filopuccio: The Bedroom

The bed's accessories

Something on which to lie down and rest; then a piece of furniture with a head, feet, mattress, bedclothes and a container for possessions . . . But even that was not enough. One needed a jug of water and a glass beside the bed; a candle or a lamp; and, before progress dismissed it, the appropriately named 'night vase', which did away with the need for disagreeable excursions into the open, or long dark retirements.

Thus accessories appeared for every kind of bedroom necessity. Soon the bed had its own table, chest of drawers, stools and chair (for those visiting an invalid), dressing-table, mirrors, shelves, and screen – indispensable to the well-conducted lady who could not be seen naked by her husband as she 'dressed' for the night.

Naturally, each accessory reflected the fashions of various cultures. Thus we move from the Empire-style bedside table now at Fontainebleau to the washstand with mirror and basin found in a South African colonial home and now in the Museum at Port Elizabeth; from the 19th-century screen in the Museum of Decorative Arts in Paris to unique objects such as the headboard of Queen Victoria's bed in Kensington Palace and the refined and precious carafes collected by two sovereigns as different as Queen Victoria and the Emperor Franz Joseph.

Queen Victoria's bedhead

Porcelain jugs and crystal bottles from Queen Victoria's room

Left: a bedside table in Empire style

A 19th-century mirror-washstand

A 19th-century screen

A 19th-century washbasin

Porcelain from Franz Joseph's room at Schönbrunn

The bed on the move

'Time is money', says the well-known proverb; and men quickly came to the conclusion that pausing in order to sleep was a waste of time and therefore of money. From which came the notion of sleeping while travelling, by contriving a bed, or something similar, on one's means of transport.

The Romans – the rich ones, at least – made much use of the carruca dormitoria, a carriage on which beds were arranged. For the rest of society it was the bottom of a wagon, softened with a scattering of straw.

The invention of new forms of travel opened up great possibilities for human ingenuity. The narrow beds and hammocks of sailing ships were the forerunners of the luxurious cabins on the great transatlantic liners of the Blue Riband era. Wagons-lits inspired a whole system ranging from the now-legendary Orient Express to the modest couchette; not to speak of coaches specially designed for the nocturnal travels of heads of state and politicians, such as the coach built for Mussolini.

There has been immense progress, too, in road travel: the bright interior of a caravan or trailer welcomes those who seek adventurous holidays, while the narrow but well-designed bunks of giant trucks afford some relief to the long-distance driver, for whom time really is money.

Bunks on a 19th-century American ship

A cabin on the transatlantic liner **Roma**

A small bed on a TIR long-distance lorry

The interior of a caravan with beds

An illustrated publicity
postcard from the
Compagnie Internationale
des Wagons-Lits,
featuring sleeping cars
and tourism

Left: The interior of a
19th-century Wagon-Lit

A compartment of the
SNCF (French National
Railways) complete with
couchettes

Below: The interior of Mussolini's railway coach

Exotic beds

Every country has its own way of using the bed. In civilizations other than the western it often lacks the rigid structural elements such as headboards, feet and bedside cupboards made of wood. These are replaced by mats, carpets and cushions strewn layer upon layer to cover, sometimes, the entire floor of the bedchamber.

It is this kind of bed that is portrayed in Indian miniatures and is represented in the Turkish bed composed of large cushions on which Sultans of the Ottoman Empire are shown in the 16th-century miniatures. It should be observed that this kind of bed, if it is in a grand reception room, comes at times to be identified with the throne upon which the sovereign reclines – a concept also found in Persia, as witness the Sun Throne in the Gulistan Palace at Teheran, which was made for the favourite of Shah Fath Ali in 1820 and was meant to be covered with carpets and cushions. What a striking contrast this unique artefact makes with the wretched pallets which in Delhi can transform the underside of a bridge into a dwelling-place!

Yet another unusual kind of bed is the hammock, originating in the Americas and already perfected there when the first European explorers landed. This is a resting-place so functional, taking up so little space and so well able to absorb pitch, toss and roll, that it was at once adopted by the conquerors' navies.

A 14th-century miniature

A miniature of 1580 portraying Murad III

An 18th-century engraving featuring a Caribbean native's hammock

Pallets under a bridge in Delhi

The Sun Throne in Gulistan Palace, Teheran

Camp bed belonging to Napoleon Bonaparte

I f the lover's bed should be air or roseleaves or swansdown, the bed of the soldier should be hard and usually is. When I joined the British Army in 1940, my winter Scottish barrack-room had neither bedsteads nor palliasses. I slept on the floor wrapped in seven blankets — far too few — and was glad when reveille sounded. I would have got up long before reveille sounded, but that would have been interpreted under Army Law as being up after lights out. When I became a sergeant I was allotted the bottom bunk of a two-tier structure in a three-stripers' dorter. The bunk above me belonged to a wizened pioneer sergeant who drank and was incontinent: he dripped aromatically on me all night long. His blankets were moist and had to be dried daily, but he would not exchange them for new: to him they were a sort of diary, or noctuary, of pleasurable potation. When I was posted to Gibraltar I became acquainted with fleas, lice and bedbugs, especially bedbugs. Putting down my head at night in the dark, I would sense that my own personal squad was marshalling for the attack; switching on the light suddenly, I would see them timorously but temporarily retreating. They would march along the floors and up the walls and over the ceiling, only to return, with the restoration of darkness, to their bloody butchery of the bed. The feet of the bedstead would be placed in cigarette-tins filled with paraffin. The bedstead itself, solid iron, would be burnt every Sunday in the yard, a Magritte-like apparition. But the bugs could not be put down. They were a nocturnal terror, all too solid despite their squashiness. They helped to put me off beds.

It was vaguely comforting to know that, thus infested, I was sharing in a pristine human condition which· a tradition of hygiene had temporarily obliterated. Certain theologians have been unwilling to accept that the condition is pristine: lice and bugs and fleas were not created by God with the rest of the fauna of Eden; they were of diabolic provenance, awaiting Adam and Eve after their expulsion. As for eliminating these small beasts, everything has been tried over the millennia — birdlime, wormwood, fires of rank hay, wolfskin cloaks (alleged, by a writer of 1585, to repel fleas, lice and bugs 'like fire'), turpentine, beer — but they are persistent lovers of humanity. The bedbug, or *cimex lectularius*, can live a whole year without food, but when it feeds it feeds; the flea, or *pulex irritans*, can leap prodigious distances away from harm. Our ancestors were more philosophical than ourselves. Samuel Pepys, the archetypal celebrator of going to bed, was always saying that — abed with Lord and Lady So-and-so and Master and Mistress Such-and-such in such-and-such an inn — the fleas 'did make us merry'. John Donne ecstasized about a flea whose 'jet walls' contained the blood of both himself and his mistress and hence was a living pledge of amorous unity.

When, as a civilian and a glutton for punishment, I went to live in Malaya, I discovered bigger bedfellows. A young hamadryad got into the bungalow, curled up upon my sleeping chest, and hissed contentedly in the human warmth. Toads normally lived in the bathroom, whence they would honk hollowly, but occasionally they would waddle through the folds of the mosquito-net and leap on to the bed. My wife woke one morning to find a toad placidly inflating his throat on her pillow. She yelled, and I told her she should kiss it and turn it back into a prince. This did not go down well. As for the mosquito-net, it did not merely fail to keep out snakes and toads: it failed to keep out mosquitoes. I sympathized (and, living on the Mediterranean as I do, still sympathize) with whole millennia of sufferers from their bites (if they can bite flesh, they can certainly bite netting). Everything has been tried to ward them off — sprigs of fern, milk mixed with hare's gall, rags dipped in honey, a boy with a night-long whisk, the closing up of casements with oiled parchment — but we have had to wait until very recently for the infallible device. This is Italian-made and consists of a small batteried machine which gives off an exact imitation of the love-call of the male mosquito. It keeps the females, which are the invariable bloodsuckers and are more intent on feeding than on love, well away.

I had in my household in Malaya a fair selection of animals — eighteen cats, twelve hens and a fine Rhode Island rooster, two rhesus monkeys, an otter with a resounding bark, a large turtle, a *musang* or civet cat, a mousedeer or *pelandok*, and the young hamadryad I have already mentioned (it entered the house wild but soon became tame enough). I woke on the morning of my birthday to find that my houseboy had let all these beasts into the bedroom to give me a special *aubade*. The cock, whose name was Regulus, monopolized the greeting.

And this brings me to the question of how best to be wakened in the morning, any morning. Few people can use a pet cockerel for the purpose; alarm clocks are cheaper and less belligerent. The earliest alarm clock was a development of the Roman *clepsydra* or water clock. A vessel placed above the sleeper's face and under the *clepsydra* would fill up with the latter's discharge during the night and overflow at dawn. A wet awakening which was also a wash. In monasteries the task of rousing the inmates was left to the sexton, but he himself had to be roused. He was in fact woken every hour by the graduated candle which King Alfred the Great had invented: tiny bells were embedded in the candle and, as the wax burned down, these would be released and fall resonantly into a metal dish.

Another method was to hang a heavy weight on a length of packthread threaded through the butt of a candle. As the candle burned to its limit the packthread too would burn, bringing the weight down with a waking crash. I remember from my childhood in northern England the more humane method of the knocker-up, who, for a halfpenny a week, hit on designated windows with a long pole. I had an uncle who gave as an excuse for being late for work that, as it had been a hot night, he had slept with his pillow on the windowsill: the knocker-up had knocked on the pillow and hence passed unheard. Another method of being knocked up was to fasten a length of twine to one's toe; this, hanging down to the street by way of the window, would be gently pulled and reveille effected. The bugle reveille, incidentally, never really worked, especially in winter. It would be ignored as one of the vague noises of the night. Soldiers are the worst wakers in the world, and who can blame them?

The true mechanical alarm clock goes back to about 1400: Chaucer died just too early to use one. The French have invented the most ingenious of these, perhaps because of royal encouragement (Louis XIII had a whole battery of such machines; Louis XIV could not drop off unless he was assured that his bedside clock was ticking). M. Musy of Paris in 1762 produced a *veilleuse* which gave subdued light all night, sounded a bell every hour, offered hot soup or coffee at any time, and clanged the sleeper awake with a fair din in the morning. In 1781 M. Morques of Marseilles invented a clock that lighted a morning candle, drew back the curtains and opened the window. Joseph Tich of Vienna devised a clock that activated its alarm with a charge of gunpowder. It is believed that Casanova, to whom prompt waking was essential when, which was often, he was not in his own bed, used one of those.

At the Great Exhibition in 1851, Mr R. W. Savage exhibited a patent Alarum Bedstead which roused the sleeper by progressively more brutal stages. A bell sounded. If that was ignored the bedclothes were mechanically whisked off. Then the mattress tilted and the sleeper was deposited on the floor. There was a more civilized variant shown at the Leipzig Fair a little later. An alarm bell sounded, then another louder one and another louder one still. Then the sleeper's nightcap was yanked off and a notice telling him to get up shoved under his nose. The last resort was mattress-tilting, but this was always palliated or palliassated by the appearance of a cup of coffee. The most neurotic of all devices was a literally travelling clock set on the mantelpiece. When it began to ring it also began to travel towards the edge and its own destruction. The waker had to give himself a mild heart attack by rushing to it and rescuing it.

The most violent wakener of all is supposed to be the cutting of the dosshouse rope. This is not really so. I slept in a London dosshouse just before World War Two – not out of need so much as curiosity – seated on a long hard bench, other dregs of humanity on either side, arms resting on the long taut rope, head resting on arms. At dawn the dosshouse master unfastened one end of the rope and we were all intended to go sprawling. But some inner mechanism woke most of us up a minute before. Or it may have been the warning yell of the master. One man lacking in that internal monitor went duly sprawling, but he did not wake. This may be regarded as the extreme of weariness.

In recounting briefly some of the engines of rousing I have assumed, and it is a very fair assumption, that most people find it hard to wake in the morning. Doctors say that this is morbid: if one has slept enough a natural rhythm will carry one, refreshed and cheerful, into the desire to get up and greet with eagerness the new day (or night, if one is on nightwork). But nobody really knows what *enough* means. Eight hours? Nine? Three? I believe that if one could do all one's sleeping upright in a chair a mere thirty minutes would suffice. Heavy after a meal, hands folded on belly, one has the sensation in a chair of gently dropping to a point of rest deep down in oneself, reaching that point, touching it an instant, and then rising again to the surface refreshed. In bed sleep always seems somehow unnatural: hard to woo, hard to be divorced from. The antiquity of the alarm clock seems to prove that this is a pristine experience; the prevalence of the instrument that it is universal.

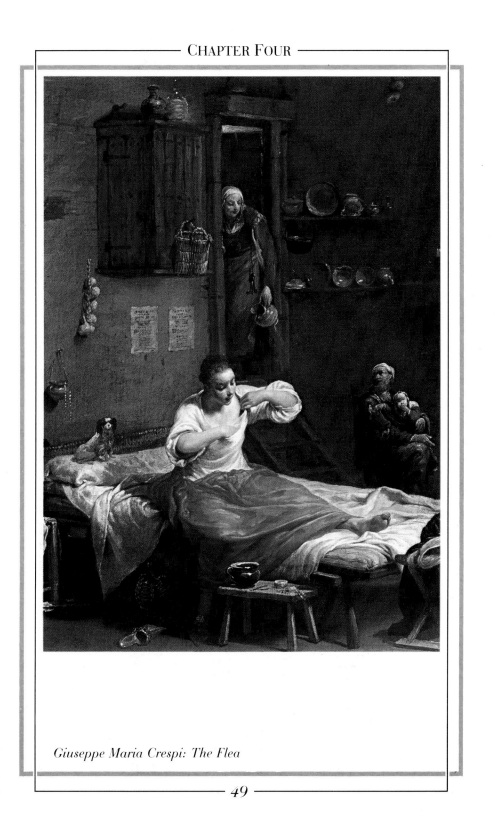

Giuseppe Maria Crespi: The Flea

Getting up and going to bed

Waking up, whether well or badly, can condition a person's mood. On the other hand, stretching one's weary body on the bed signifies closing the day, and preparing oneself to enjoy the serenity of sleep. Both are moments when we are briefly alone with ourselves. But it has not always been so: in the Middle Ages, for example (the detail from Gentile da Fabriano's painting bears witness to this), those who lived in lordly dwellings rose and went to bed assisted by servants and maids. In the Renaissance and in subsequent centuries, the levée *was ruled by a rigid ceremonial which ordained every move by the servants and courtiers around their lord's bed.*

With the arrival of the romantic spirit, people returned to the notion of privacy, and the image of woman came into prominence, idealized but also given a subtle fascination which the 19th-century nightgown does not hide. Finally, we consider the moment of going to bed as being that in which one approaches love (see the Art Nouveau illustration from a Balzac novel).

For children, bedtime should be a moment of sweetness, as they are snugly tucked up by their mother. Yet for some, such as the little foundling in the painting by Cayley-Robinson, this reassuring sweetness has to remain an unattainable myth.

Jean Francois Raffaelli: Le réveil

Overleaf: Pseudo-Marcula (?): Cosimo Riccardi visiting Gian Gastone de' Medici

Casas: La mandra

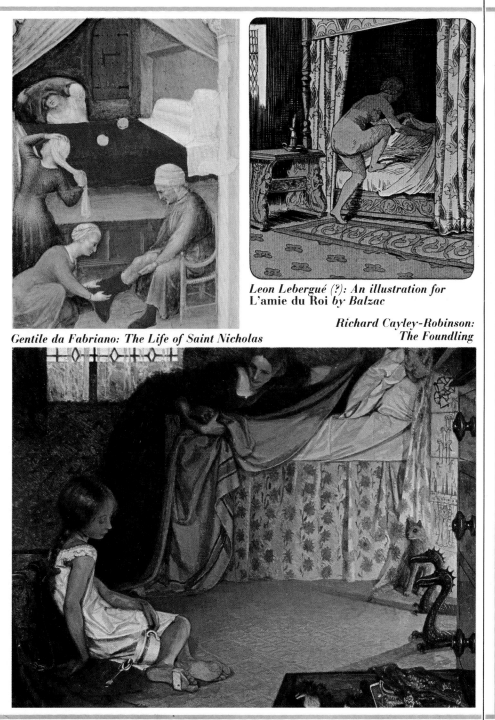

Leon Lebergué (?): An illustration for
L'amie du Roi by Balzac

Richard Cayley-Robinson:
The Foundling

Gentile da Fabriano: The Life of Saint Nicholas

The bed and sex

It is difficult to imagine love without a bed. Even in the Kama Sutra, *that somewhat pedantic treatise on the art of making love, most of the techniques described require a bed — not to mention extraordinarily athletic participants — if they are to be performed successfully.*

Even when Indian teaching about sex does not follow the Tantric way (which uses it as a means of spiritual elevation), it still allows preeminence to the act of love. Erotic sculpture and painting similar to the art of Ajanta is found in many other places. The Japanese, too, have created prints which capture the most intimate anatomical detail in an exquisite manner.

Western culture is more conservative in this respect: paintings often conceal an erotic theme behind a screen of myth (as in the detail from The Love of Mars and Venus*), or treat it in a generalized way, as in the miniature from the* Theatrum Sanitatis.

Only at the end of the 18th century was prudery set aside — the painting by Jean Frederic Schall is significant. In the late 19th-century photograph of an American prostitute the bed has become almost a method of advertisement; while it is transformed into the star performer, a symbol to unchain fantasy, in the Art Nouveau design of 1902, which illustrates a novel by Balzac.

Leon Lebergué (?): An illustration for L'amie du Roi *by Balzac*

Isoda Koryusai: Shunga, or Images of Spring

A fresco from Cave Seventeen at Ajanta

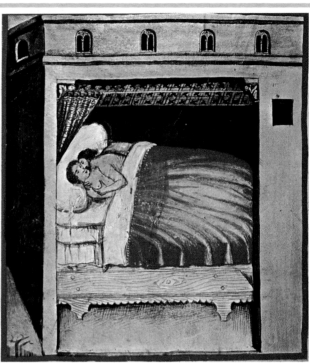

Theatrum Sanitatis: Erotic Scene
Palazzo di Schifanoia: The Love of Mars and Venus

Jean Frederic Schall:
La soubrette officieuse

An American prostitute

Jean Huber: Le lever de Voltaire à Ferney

W aking is one thing, getting out of bed quite another. The traditional torment is not opening one's eyes (though it is astonishing how one's eyes, once shut, long to remain so) but engaging the world again. In the old days, before bedrooms were heated, to get out of one's winter bed was to meet excruciating cold. One is never warmer than in bed, and the warmth is all of one's own making. True, it can be primed artificially with a hot water bottle or a warming pan, but it ends self-engendered, a genuine achievement and not one to give up lightly. To be unwilling to get up may be to recall the perfectly tempered warmth of the womb; the cold out there is more than a matter of temperature; it is an aspect of the iron hardness of the cruel world, hostile to the quivering nakedness of soul as well as body. Lying down, limbs relaxed, we have come to terms with gravity. Getting up, we lift our bodies painfully in opposition to it. Never stand when you can sit, went the old soldier's adage; never sit when you can lie down. You can do a lot of useful things lying down, or half-lying down, or half sitting up. Why should we confront exterior cold in order to study, write books, or govern a country? Evelyn Waugh, in his *Sword of Honour* trilogy, presents Winston Churchill as issuing orders for the administration of an embattled empire 'from a deep bed in a deep shelter'. If he could do that, we at least can conduct, as far as techniques permit, a fair number of important activities undressed and between blankets.

It has been suggested several times that a good way

of conserving fuel in winter would be to decree an occasional working week in bed for all bureaucrats, journalists and others whose labours are chiefly to do with paper and telephones. True manual work — in the sense of digital operations unpowered by arm muscle — is possible enough in bed, but there are some jobs unsuited to a posture of relaxation. Nevertheless, I once knew a very idle man who languidly chopped wood in bed, and I have heard of an eccentric lady – the famous the Hon. Blanche T. – who milked a cow there (this was a prize Jersey who would submit only to manipulations of her mistress). The kneading of bread is a bed-activity of Rumanian winters, and bedridden ladies may sew and knit, but these touch the region of art. Art of any kind is suitable for the blankets except sculpture of the Michelangelesque sort.

Fantin-Latour used to draw in bed, wearing an overcoat and scarf and a top hat: at least, that is how Whistler has depicted him. The desire which G. K. Chesterton had of drawing on the ceiling with a long coloured pencil while bulkily lying was, in fact, fulfilled in the later life of Matisse. He, in old age, as Cecil Beaton has recorded, used to draw on his bedside walls with bits of charcoal affixed to a long cane. I have read that William Morris imported a handloom into his bedroom, but there seems no account of his having woven anything there. John Milton, as is well known, composed *Paradise Lost* in bed, and then sent for one or other of his daughters to transcribe the day's quota of lines. He was blind, of course, and would have benefited from Braille, which, for the blind or sighted, is a great invention when applied to books under the blanket. Thomas Hobbes drew geometrical problems on the sheets or on his own naked thighs. Samuel Johnson, when a Grub Street writer, was forced to produce his small histories and pamphlets in bed for lack of a fire: he cut holes in the blankets for his hands.

Musical composition is possible in bed, unless one has reached the monumental phase of the orchestral score, which requires a lectern and an upright posture. Rossini composed many of his operas from the pillows. On one occasion, finishing a duet for an opera to open that very night, he let the manuscript fall on the floor. Too lazy or comfortable to get up to retrieve it, he wrote the duet again. It was radically different from the first version. I heard of a composer whose wife suffered from dermatographia – a condition of the skin which enables fingers to draw or write on it in the expectation that the imprint will not disappear for an hour or more. One night a theme came to him. He lacked pencil and paper. I need not go on.

The world is for the most part so puritanical that it will not accept the conjunction of bed and work. When the postman comes to deliver parcels (always of books for review or unpaid commendation) at eleven in the morning, he says reprovingly: 'Ah, well, some of us have to work.' This is because he is in uniform and has been up for hours. I myself, though in bed, may well have completed a thousand words of prose by that time. But there is apparently an intrinsic virtue in being up. We are both men of letters, but he is the real worker. I knew a retired general who insisted on the healthfulness of early rising.

He would get up at his house in Sevenoaks at six, bath, shave, eat breakfast, then take a train to Charing Cross. From there he would take a taxi to his club in Pall Mall and sleep there in the library – with a brief interval for luncheon – until it was time to take the train home again. To sleep fully dressed in a club armchair had, for him, the properties of a laudable activity. I am writing this dressed and shaven, seated on a hard chair. I could have done the work better in bed, but I have grown sensitive to the postman's censure.

The hero of Goncharov's story, Oblomov (the man whose servant asked 'And what would sleep be without bugs?'), is taken to be the patron saint of all who hate getting up. But he stands for Russian negativity, whereas bed is for cubatory action. It is hard for the unimaginative to conceive that a person may lie in bed, without pencil or paper and indeed with eyes closed, and be creating important art or science. One art in particular, a very modern one, can only be practised in its initial phase by the artist's sending himself to bed and closing his eyes. This is the art of the film or television scenario. The scenarist must lie down in the dark and watch the film unroll in the projection room of his skull. Analogously, a symphony must be composed in the brain and heard there, down to the last drum thump and tuba blast, before it can be committed to scoring paper. This is the way Sibelius worked. Einstein lay down one day and saw $E = Mc^2$ flash in fire on the interior of his eyelids. In bed, as Delmore Schwartz might have put it, begin responsibilities.

Dimitri Kessel: photograph of Matisse at work

The bed in painting after 1700

Artists have painted people in bed throughout history, but, before the 18th century, with a certain caution. When the subjects were women, dressed scantily or not at all, the painter needed an excuse, so his portrait had to represent Venus or some other sacred character of religion or mythology. But after 1700 there was a radical change. The reclining female now became a recognized artistic device. Not surprisingly, once the female subject ceased to be a goddess and became a real person, she was often placed on a real, everyday bed, and engaged in ordinary bed-pursuits – rest, love, abandon, indolence, lust.

Earlier paintings, such as Goya's Naked Maja, *continue some of the traditions of goddesses and myths, and even the Olympia painted by both Manet and Cézanne was in a sense a legendary figure. But the draped nudes which inspired later painters were ordinary women. They can be seen in Renoir's many luminous figures, or Gaugin's work in Tahitian exile, or in the pictures of Suzanne Valadon, a woman painter in the bohemian Paris of the Impressionists, or finally in Chagall's draped nude, who is actually his own wife in bed.*

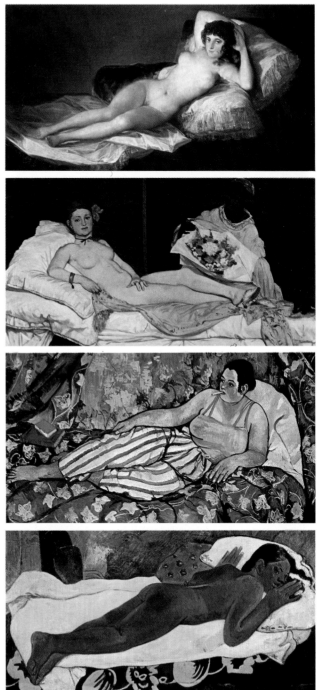

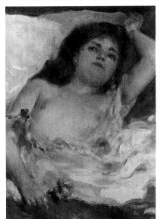

Auguste Renoir: The Rose

Left:
Francisco Goya: The Naked Maja
Edouard Manet: Olympia
Suzanne Valadon: The Blue Room
Paul Gauguin: Tahitian with Idol

Marc Chagall: To My Wife

Paul Cézanne: Olympia

The beds of famous people

The public buildings and private houses of Europe and America are stuffed with beds in which slept Napoleon, or Garibaldi, or Frederick the Great, or Washington, or Simon Bolivar . . . an abundance unconnected with the fact that few things give a better idea of a person than his bed. Not, of course, the bed in which he slept for one night in transit, but that of his habitual residence, chosen by him and surrounded by the distinctive atmosphere of his own taste.

Franz Joseph is reflected in the thoroughly bourgeois room he shared with Elizabeth of Bavaria, and even more clearly in the camp bed which, in the luxury of Schönbrunn, was his favourite resting place.

George Washington at Mount Vernon rediscovered his own dimension as a colonial and a countryman.

The royal beds of Hampton Court and Chambord testify to the pomp and ceremony in which were lived out the 'official' lives of Queen Mary Tudor (1553–58) and Francis I of France (1515–47).

The bed of Charles-Louis of Bourbon-Parma, King of Étruria (1803–7), shows how aristocrats of minor lineage also amassed luxury. What a contrast with the modest bedroom of Florence Nightingale at Claydon House, her English country home!

Florence Nightingale's bedroom at Clayton House

Mary Tudor's bedroom at Hampton Court

Charles-Louis's bed The bed of Francis I at Chambord George Washington's bed

The bedroom of Franz Joseph and Elizabeth at Schönbrunn

The bed in tragedy

We think of bed as a place of rest, but it has often been a place of violence or a focus of tragedy. Othello – the most archetypal of tragedies – turns around a bed of passion, which is transformed by treachery and jealousy into a place of unmerited execution. Bed, because it is a place where abandon is normal, is also the ideal stage for tragic deaths or noble suicides. Hence Cato, who chose to kill himself in bed rather than see Julius Caesar triumph; hence Cleopatra putting the asp to her breast in bed; hence King Sardanapalus gathering his wives into his flaming bed-chamber rather than surren-der Nineveh to the Medes. What better place for a noble suicide than bed?

By contrast, bed may be a haven of rest and inner tran-quility brutally and dramati-cally desecrated by violence, as it was when Lucretia was raped by Tarquin in her own bedchamber; when Alexander de' Medici was murdered in bed in 1537 by his own cousin Lorenzino; and when Wallen-stein was surprised by hired assassins in his bedroom.

Anonymous, 17th century: The Death of Wallenstein

Delacroix The Death of Sardan apalus

Delacroix: The Death of Cato

Anon 15 century: The Rap of Lucretia by Sextu Tarquin

Castagnola: The Death of Alexander de' Medici
Guercino (Giovanni Francesco Barbieri): Cleopatra

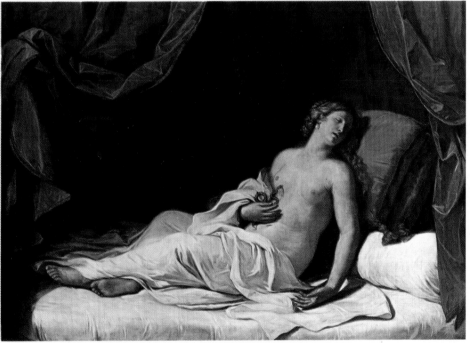

Anon: The Funeral of Anne of Britanny

As one gets older, the thing which I am at present getting, one starts to associate bed less with birth and love and life than with death. Nor is bed just the place where one is reasonably deposited to get on, in as much relaxation as possible, with the business of dying. Bed is sometimes the unreasonable begetter of death. Many old people, pulses beating healthful enough music, stomachs purring with the pleasure of a good supper, put off the hour of going to bed and prefer to sleep in a chair – doze, rather, with one eye half-open for the hovering dark angel. People do not usually die in chairs – other than electric ones – unless they are like the nonagenarian French gourmande who whispered to the waiter: *'Le dessert, vite – je me sens passer.'* But to die in one's bed asleep is all too common. It is perhaps a good thing. It does not disturb other sleepers. But it frustrates the human desire to remain curious about the nature of what Henry James called the great distinguished thing.

The fact that one can not only die in one's sleep but become seriously ill during it seems to give the lie to the assumption that sleep is a healthy activity, or passivity. If one can wake up raging with influenza, or with dangerous-looking maculae on the skin, or half-paralytic, then some noxious forces have been at work on a body unprotected by the strong carapace of consciousness. I always wake in a bed exhausted, though never in a chair, and I know why. The schoolmaster consciousness has been out of the classroom and the disruptive atomies of the dark have been left to their book-tearing and ink-throwing. Ghastly psychoneural dramas have been enacting themselves, and there has been no stage manager to order the descent of the curtain. I have been scared, my heart has been thumping to the limit, I am covered in unwholesome sweat. Everybody, whether a sufferer from nightmares or not, wakes up exhausted. Sleep in a bed is evidently not necessarily a good thing.

The link between life and death is illness, and the bed of sickness, as opposed to convalescence, is the wheel of fire that Shakespeare mentions in *King Lear*. Its terrors can be mitigated only by making it a bed in a hospital ward, when it becomes highly functional, unassociable with sexual pleasure, and indeed set around with so much banal discomfort that illness has no chance to be exalted to noble agony and classical terror. Sheets and coverlet are very plain and are so tucked in as to evoke ancestral memories of chains and straps and other stabilizers premonitory of torture. The processes of bodily excretion have to be fulfilled in impossible vessels. One is awakened at an unreasonable hour, in order that the hospital routine, which never consults the superficial welfare of the patients, may function like the heartless machine it is. At dawn, or foredawn even, the interests of health may be subverted. I remember once being made to get up in black London December and go out to a newsagent not yet open, there to wait shivering so that I could buy the ward's copies of the *Daily Mirror*. The following day I was due to be investigated for a possible cerebral tumour.

The only thing that can be said for being dangerously ill in a hospital is that it is not conducive to dying quietly: it raises the pulse rate with anger and resentment, fires the system with combative adrenalin, and makes one determined to outlive one's white-clad oppressors. The only decent hospital that ever seems to have existed was the one in Milan where the young Ernest Hemingway was the only patient and was tended by a superfluity of beautiful nurses who had nothing to do but fall in love with him. But, human nature being so adaptable, we are all capable of learning to love what we loathe, and I have seen grown men cry because they were cured and had to leave the sick friends they had made. For a hospital ward is a genuine bedbound community, a one-sexed club where the only qualification is disease and there is always disease to talk about. It is not static, like the Athenaeum, since the members change back to health or move on to death or permanent philosophical impairment at a rate unknown to Pall Mall. There are moments of fearful excitement, when the examining cortège comes in. There is harmless sexual perturbation, since the uniform makes most nurses beautiful. Visitors from the outside world are more tolerated than welcomed: healthy, they do not belong to the club.

You resign your membership by being discharged fit or wheeled out dead. To see this latter happen to men you have spoken to, laughed with, given a furtive cigarette, depresses temporarily but does not frighten. It is given to all men once to die, and to process the dead briskly and without sentimentality is one of the functions of the hospital. We foresee our own deaths the more easily, and the more easily reconcile ourselves to them, by being in a place where death is pertinent and part of daily life. And I think most of us do in fact take comfort in foreseeing death in a hospital. John Betjeman, the Poet Laureate, is specific in conjuring his latter end in a *cottage* hospital. None of us wants to die at home. We do not want to defile the bed of happiness and discord and give our relicts the trouble of trundling our bones down the stairs. Preferably we would wish to die in a duel, a battle, a street mugging, or in the act of trying to assassinate a great public enemy, but a hospital bed — not being really a bed but a machine to accommodate an impersonal sick organism — will do as a second best.

Anon: Hospital Scene

Dreams and nightmares

We spend almost a third of our lives in bed asleep, and often in sleep all rational thought is suspended, and the fears, joys and anxieties of the day re-emerge oppressively and tumultuously in the form of dreams and nightmares. In the past, people attributed great importance to dreams. They looked upon them as divine warnings and had interpreters ready to explain their significance. We, in the modern world, have psychoanalysis and its prophets Freud and Jung.

In the art of every age there has been a strong temptation to take inspiration from dreams and to try to capture nocturnal fantasies in artistic form. Sometimes the artist has to follow the narrow path of saintly chastity, as when Simone Martini painted Saint Martin's dreams in his record of the Saint's life in the Basilica of Saint Francis of Assisi, or in the miniature dedicated to insomnia in the Theatrum Sanitatis. At other times painters are led to depict erotic fantasies, which may be camouflaged by myth and legend, like The Dream of Solomon *by Luca Giordano, or may take a neo-classical form, like* Le sommeil *by Gustave Courbet. More recently, efforts have been made to portray the reality of dreams (in so far as dreams can be real) in paintings like the erotic and disturbing* Nightmare *by Füssli or the surrealistic* Venus endormie *by Paul Delvaux.*

Luca Giordano: The Dream of Solomon

Paul Delvaux: Venus endormie

Simone Martini: The Dream of Saint Martin

Theatrum Sanitatis: Insomnia

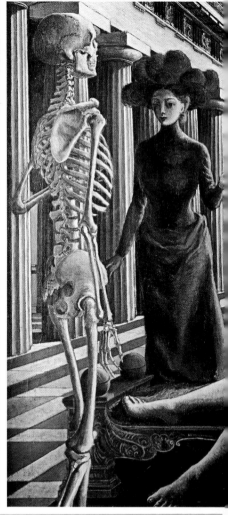

Gustave Courbet: Le sommeil
Overleaf: Toulouse-Lautrec: In Bed (detail)

Johann Heinrich Füssli: The Nightmare

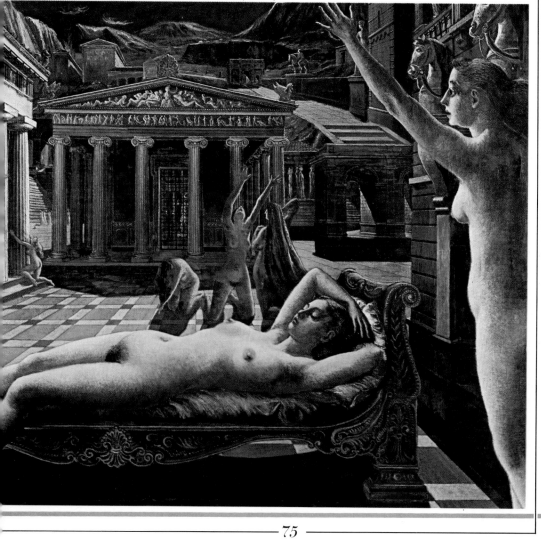

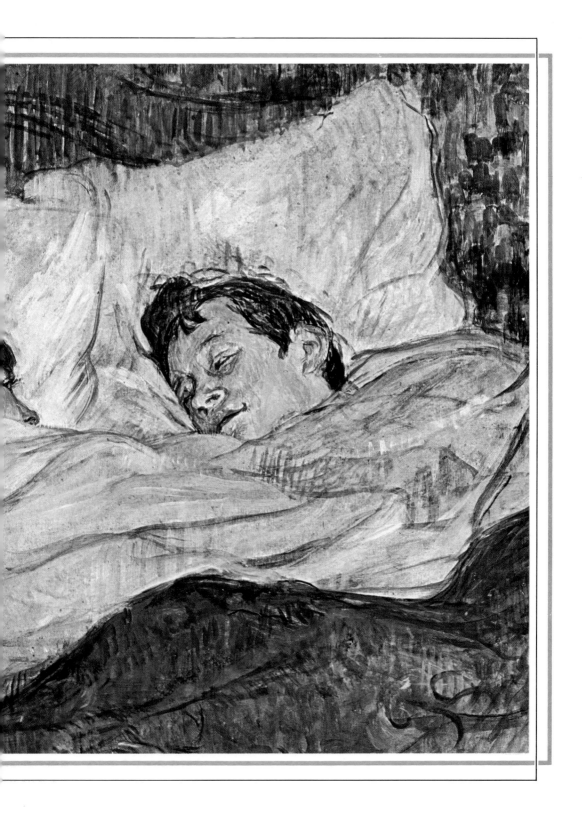

Arthur Rackham:
Children Sleeping

Trautl Conrad:
Opening the
Christmas Stockings

Anon: Hush-a-bye, Baby,
on the Tree Top

Anon: Little Red Riding Hood

Tommaso Minardi: Self-portrait

One of the few things the world knows about William Shakespeare is that he bequeathed his second-best bed to his widow. This has been taken to signify a desire to hurt and humiliate: why not the best bed? The reason is simple. Shakespeare's daughter Susannah and her husband Dr John Hall would inherit the great house called New Place in Stratford, and they would naturally occupy the master bedroom where the best bed lay. Ann Shakespeare, the widow, was put in the position of dowager entitled to the next best bed in the house – not the third or fourth best. The bed on which Ann was to lie was probably the one upon which she and Will had dreamed youthful dreams and consummated their love. When he grew rich he bought a better bed, more apt for distinguished guests than for the marital routine, but this other one, now second-best, carried a large canopy of hope and was stuffed with the roseleaves of memory.

We take it for granted that a bed, or a series of beds, should be among the prized possessions of a man who has made his way. The traditional difference between the exalted and the humble is figured as much in sleeping arrangements as in plate and cutlery and the contents of the garage or stable. The very low have always slept on the floor, or, at their very lowest, on the street; at their least low the low have possessed only a portable couch or charpoy. When, in the New Testament, a cured cripple is told to take up his bed and walk, we are surprised into realizing that that basic bed for all men is the light watchman's truckle, on which the Sikhs of the East still snore. In Shakespeare's time, as before, the gorgeous bed was the true symbol of achieved gentility. It had carved posts and a tester, a canopy and curtains. It was, when you come to think of it, a kind of proleptic tomb. When Macbeth speaks of sleep as being the death of each day's life, he is voicing the Elizabethan gentleman's approach to burying himself in bed. Here lies Master William Shakespeare, or some other man with the same name.

Our attitude to bed-going is much more casual. We do not dress ourselves up in a kind of shroud, as former ages did, and don a nightcap (a nightcap is now reserved for drinking). An increasing number of people sleep naked, which seems to imply a return to the womb rather than an anticipation of the tomb. We do not step into a darkness made by heavy curtains: we like the odd glimpse of light from the sky or street, an assurance that life is going on out there, quietly, in a diminished form, ready to burst into tomorrow's sun and birdsong. Napoleon insisted on sleeping in total blackness, an occlusion which Josephine could not stand. This is probably typical of the imperial mind, this willingness to enter the city of dreadful night. A monarch is himself the sun, as Louis XIV made clear. When his bed-curtains are drawn back, he permits the light to initiate a new day.

I think the time has come to make a confession. I am writing about beds, and yet I have not used a bed for the last six years. Of course, I must rush in at once with a qualification. I have, in fact, slept in many beds, but these have been in hotels, on ships, and in other people's houses. In my own house there is no bed, merely a mattress on the floor. This, being a place reserved for rest, sleep, love, writing, reading, listening to music, and other activities or non-activities which make no direct contribution to the wealth of the world, may well be considered to be a bed as we have so far, without tedium of definition, understood it, but most people's notion of bedhood is more exalted. Literally so. A bed, or rather a bedstead (compare home and homestead), is a raised structure. You get into it or on to it in a fairly dignified manner. You lower your body to a sitting position and then raise your legs to a lying position. If you sleep on the floor you crawl to your rest like a beast or drop heavily upon it like a clown. In this latter case your legs, meeting the resilience of the mattress, involuntarily go up into the air. This is not dignified. It is not even human. Nevertheless, I have come to prefer the mattress on the floor to the true bed, and for a variety of reasons.

In the first place, you cannot fall out of it. You are already, so to speak, fallen, and you can go no lower. In my time I have been a great faller out of beds, and than falling out of beds I know of no experience more traumatic. It always happens, of course, when you are asleep, and the shock to the system is considerable. As I roll a good deal in my sleep, and I do not like to have the bedclothes tucked in, I am naturally more subject to falling than the sleeper who lies as in death. I have also, by chance or destiny, been allotted sleeping partners given to kicking in their sleep. In addition to the pet animals I have already mentioned, I had a Siamese cat which insisted on lying between my human partner and myself. This cat did not much care for me, and it used its entire battery of offence to get me out of bed. Place an entire zoo between myself and my present bedmate, and, though I may be assaulted, I cannot properly be dislodged. From mattress to floor, when the mattress is on the floor, there is no fall.

In the second place, if your sleeping area is at ground level, you are able to surround yourself with the appurtenancies of relaxation in a manner impossible if you are limited to a bedside table. You can have a whole library spread on the floor, a tea-making apparatus, a digital clock with built-in bugle call, a record-player, tape-recorder and large radio, a portable musical instrument (not a piano but certainly a piano-accordion), a medicine chest, a wide selection of strong drinks, even a small refrigerator. All the cubatory pleasures of the world, and no need to reach far to grasp them.

In the third place, not having bought a bed you have saved money. To be honest, this was not a consideration when I moved to where I now am living, meaning mostly lying on the floor. A double bed was in the remover's van, but the local police would not permit that van to be parked in order that the process of moving could be consummated. I had to send this van into the open country, buy a small property nearby, and have the furniture transferred thereto. I have not yet slept in that property, but I understand that all the furniture is safe though dusty, including the double bed. I doubt if I shall ever sleep in that bed again.

Now consider what I take to be the primary characteristic of the bedstead — the fact that it is raised from the floor. I can see no utilitarian rationale in this: to raise the bed does not prevent small creatures of the night from getting into it; it makes it easier for your enemies to stab you than if you were on the floor. I can see the low comedy potentialities of a space beneath the bed — the chamberpot to be clanged by the comedian's boot; the lover in hiding who finds himself next to another lover in hiding; the burglar of the old maid's fantasy. I can only attribute this raising of the bed to, say, crotch height to the origin of the bed as a symbol of overlordship. I, the king, am high; you, the retainers, must rest with the blackbeetles and the ashes of the dead fire. In my youth I was acquainted (this is myself speaking, not some imaginary monarch) with young Marxists who lived in hovels and, needless to say, did not possess even a mattress. They used to assert, among other things, that a bed was a bourgeois property and hence to be eliminated from the coming classless society. Very old-fashioned talk.

But if we examine, however cursorily, the history of the bed, we shall find that it was, for whole millennia, unintended for the likes of me. Go to the house of Meryre, the high priest of Tel-el-Amarna in Egypt, and you will find many halls and chambers but only one bedroom. Here, at the very beginning of the history of sleep, in Egypt the mother of our arts, we see the basic bed patterns of the autocratic West. The bed of priest or monarch was a masterpiece of craft. Commoners either slept on the floor or else on a light charpoy. Queen Hetep-Heres, about 2690 BC, has left behind the gold plating of her bed, though its core of wood has perished. The legs are the legs of lions and the joints of the whole elaborate structure are sheathed in copper. There were curtains, and they were probably (vainly, always vainly) designed to keep mosquitoes away. Tutankhamen, circa 1350 BC, had beds of ivory and gold-sheathed teak with headrests of lapis lazuli and turquoise. We may divine that kings and queens did not sleep any better on their ornate machines than peasants on their mud floors (Shakespeare is always going on about this), but the elaboration of a bed had nothing to do with som-niference. It was all a matter of symbolism — weight, dignity, immovability. In other words, the kingly bed anticipated the kingly tomb, and even hinted at the possibility of resurrection. The solemnity of a monarch's going to bed foretold the glory of his obsequies.

I need not emphasize the essential vulgarity of this glorification of a mere couch of unconsciousness. The expenditure of gold and skill on the quotidian royal tomb was sickening enough in the past, but it has reached its nauseous limit in our own century, chiefly among orien-tal potentates who have forgotten their native culture and learned from the West only ingenuity and display. I am thinking of the maharajah whose bedposts were four naked goddesses sculpted in silver, from whose nipples there spurted, on the pressing of a button near the pillow, various raw nightcaps and whose arms by clockwork were made to wield fans. I am thinking of the Malay sultan I recently visited whose canopied bed is also a pornographic cinema. For God's sake give me the floor.

Let no reader speak of sour grapes. It is true that, all through my childhood and adolescence, I never had a good bed in a good bedroom. As a stepchild I envied the situation of the archetypal stepchild Cinderella, who at least slept warm in a kitchen lively with friendly mice. For I was always up in the cold boxroom or garret, and my bed, which preceded me on move after move, was a creaking rusty iron abomination, intricately reticulated, with ancient dust trapped in the decussations. The network sagged and so did the stained lumpy mattress spread on it. But my rejection of a bedstead in late middle age can be justified wholly by reason and the consultation of the higher, or lower, comfort.

Leon Carré (?): Miniature for A Thousand and One Nights Illustrating the Tale of King Omar

The communal bed

Architects call a bed the 'minimum habitat', the least space needed for a dwelling for one person. Hence it is the basic unit around which any communal building intended to house a large number of people in a limited space must be designed, whether it be a hospital, prison, college, hotel, barracks, or whatever. In these buildings a bed is not simply a person's place of rest, but also his home, and almost everyone, in such circumstances, will try to give this territory a special, personal character, however anonymous his surroundings may be.

In a prison cell, the bed is the one basic piece of furniture (see the cell in the Castel Sant' Angelo). It can become a table, sofa, or even an embroidery frame, as it did for the Neapolitan noblewoman Luisa Sanfelice during the months of anguish she spent in prison, waiting for her death sentence to be carried out.

Then there is another kind of cell: the picture of the Charterhouse of Serra San Bruno shows that a simple bed was almost the only furniture in a Carthusian monk's solitary cell. By contrast, the beds in hospitals, workhouses and orphanages were crowded together and the horror and pathos of these institutions can be glimpsed in the military hospital of Scutari, where Florence Nightingale worked in the Crimean War, and in the asylum at Arles where Van Gogh spent many sad days.

A cell at the time of Gregory XVI at Castel Sant' Angelo

Gioacchino Toma: Luisa Sanfelice in Prison

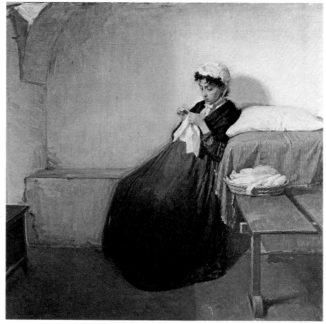

A cell in the Charterhouse of Serra San Bruno

A ward in the military hospital at Scutari

Small beds in an orphanage

Vincent van Gogh: The Hospital in Arles

The bed, illness and death

Birth, rest, love – but also illness and death: bed is the background to the Seven Ages of Man. In its aspect of 'bed of sorrow' it is purely functional. The bed becomes the centre of activity devoted to the invalid in attempts to satisfy his every need. Visiting the sick has been a subject for illustration from the earliest times. Antique miniatures (those of the Theatrum Sanitatis go back to the 14th century): illustrations of biblical stories: heavily sentimental paintings like those of Greuze: these all portray the sharing of others' sufferings.

As a 'death bed' rather than a 'bed of sorrow', the bed becomes an altar, around which family and friends gather piously, to give solemnity to the dying person's last moments on earth and to emphasize the Christian significance of his entrance into life eternal. This is very well expressed by the Master of the Holy Cross in the Death of Saint Clare, *which makes a striking contrast with the remoteness and coldness of Mantegna's Dead Christ – truly a symbol of death. Before death all men are equal: rich and poor, old and young, ignorant and cultured. Not even the luminaries of medicine can escape – the celebrated French anatomist Bichat died at only thirty-one.*

Anonymous miniature: Jacob Falls Sick

Theatrum Sanitatis: Visit to the Sick

Master of the Holy Cross: Death of Saint Clare

Anonymous: Bichat Dying   *Jean-Baptiste Greuze: Le fils puni*

Andrea Mantegna: The Dead Christ

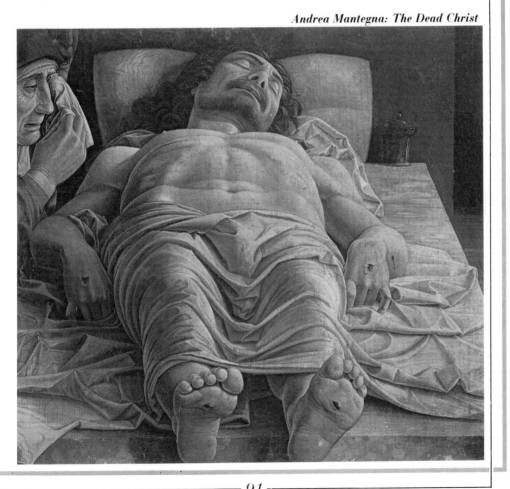

Above: Detail of the Bazaar of Marrakesh
Below: Le Douanier Rousseau: La bohémienne endormie

In sleep we all become the same, and where we sleep is a profound irrelevancy. I still do not know why we sleep. It cannot be to rest the mind and the body, since the body is far more exhausted on waking than on lying down, and the mind whirls madly in sleep in extravagant but quite useless phantasmagorias. What I am told however, leaving me little the wiser, is that the accumulation in the blood of acid waste products of the functional activity of the muscles and nervous system results in a gradually increasing loss of irritability in the brain cells. This insensitivity to stimuli finally results in a depression of their activity sufficient to cause unconsciousness. Another theory is that during waking hours the brain cells use up their oxygen store faster than it can be replaced by absorption of oxygen from the blood, and that this oxygen starvation, which can only be reversed by unconsciousness, is another diminutioner of cellular irritability. It seems a poor description of being awake – suffering from, or rejoicing in, irritability of the cells. There is also the Neuron Theory, which says that afferent impulses reach the cortical cells through the contact of the terminal arborizations of afferent nerve fibres with the dendritic processes of the cells. These latter processes are contractile, we are told, and their retraction mechanically produces sleep by constituting a rupture in the path of the afferent impulses, which isolates the cortical cells from external stimuli. You will be pleased to know that this dendritic retraction has not yet been histologically demonstrated. There are also certain anaemia theories about sleep (rhythmical loss of tone in the vasomotor centre in the medulla, stronger and stronger stimulations needed to maintain normal tone, effect of their action on blood pressure insufficient to maintain adequate brain blood flow: result unconsciousness). The mere summarization of these theories is enough to induce sleep.

All we really know is that sleep is a fact of life, but only a fact of the life of the individual. Aldous Huxley, in his series of lectures called *The Human Situation*, points out justly that social organizations never sleep: they 'live, so to speak, in a state of chronic insomnia; they never depart from themselves nor open themselves up to new accessions of life and insight.' Huxley is all for sleep as a sure mode of escape from the ego: 'It is a beautiful thought that even a Hitler, even a Himmler, even a Genghis Khan . . . can forget for a moment his fearful daytime preoccupations.' Church and State cannot draw on the blissful reserves of the unconscious: that is why they tend to stupidity and evil. What both Church and State are skilful at, however, is the creation of monstrous bedsteads like the House of Commons and Westminster Abbey. These, of course, are also tombs.

Let us forget beds and allow Robert Louis Stevenson, who sleeps, the hunter home from the hill, in Samoa, to tell us what sleep should be:

> Night is a dead monotonous period under a roof: but in the open world it passes lightly, with its stars and dews and perfumes, and the hours are marked by changes in the face of Nature. What seems a kind of temporal death to people choked between walls and curtains, is only a light and living slumber to the man who sleeps a-field. All night long

he can hear Nature breathing deeply and freely; even as she takes rest, she turns and smiles; and there is one stirring hour unknown to those who dwell in houses, when a wakeful influence goes abroad over the sleeping hemisphere, and all the outdoor world are on their feet. It is then that the cock first crows, not this time to announce the dawn, but like a cheerful watchman speeding the course of night. Cattle awake on the meadows; sheep break their fast on dewy hillsides, and change to a new lair among the ferns; and houseless men, who have lain down with the fowls, open their dim eyes and behold the beauty of the night.

In other words, sleep is healthiest when it is aware of the movement of the earth, the passage of the stars, the flow of the rivers. Moses in his *moïse* saw the light filtered down through the gaps in the osier weave and was vaguely conscious of the movement of the waters which bore him to his destiny. Only tyrants seek stasis and the dark, the simulacrum of the tomb past which adulators file. The study of sleep is wonder; the study of beds is fear.

Vincent van Gogh: The Artist's Bedroom in Arles